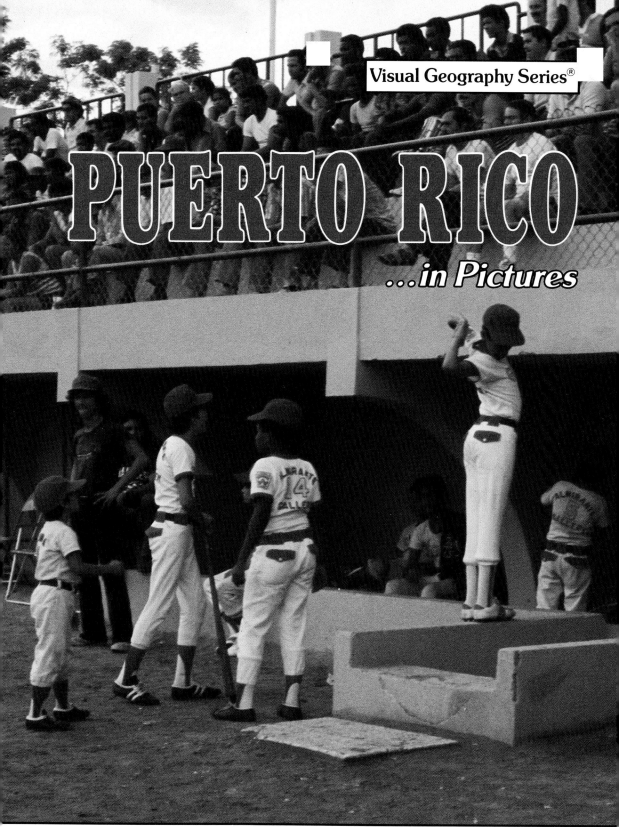

Visual Geography Series®

PUERTO RICO

...in Pictures

Prepared by
Geography Department

Lerner Publications Company
Minneapolis

Independent Picture Service

A friendly game of dominoes is in progress in a San Juan
square.

This book is an all-new edition in the Visual Geography Series. Previous editions were published by
Sterling Publishing Company, New York City. The
text, set in 10/12 Century Textbook, is fully revised
and updated, and new photographs, maps, charts, and
captions have been added.

LIBRARY OF CONGRESS CATALOGING-IN-PUBLICATION DATA

Puerto Rico in pictures.

(Visual geography series)
Includes index.
Summary: Introduces the topography, history, soci-
ety, economy, and governmental structure of Puerto
Rico.
1. Puerto Rico. [1. Puerto Rico] I. Series: Visual
geography series (Minneapolis, Minn.).
F1958.P8778   1987   972.95   86–33746
ISBN 0-8225-1821-X (lib. bdg.)

International Standard Book Number: 0-8225-1821-X
Library of Congress Card Catalog Number: 86-33746

VISUAL GEOGRAPHY SERIES®

Publisher
Harry Jonas Lerner
Associate Publisher
Nancy M. Campbell
Executive Series Editor
Mary M. Rodgers
Editorial Assistant
Nora W. Kniskern
Illustrations Editor
Nathan A. Haverstock
Consultants/Contributors
Dr. Ruth F. Hale
Nathan A. Haverstock
Sandra K. Davis
Designer
Jim Simondet
Cartographer
Carol F. Barrett
Indexer
Kristine S. Schubert
Computer Systems Consultant
Rhona H. Landsman
Production Manager
Gary J. Hansen

Courtesy of Puerto Rico Federal Affairs Administration

Rich aquatic life and the clarity of Puerto Rico's coastal
waters make snorkeling an ideal sport for all ages.

Acknowledgments

Title page photo courtesy of Puerto Rican Federal Affairs Administration.

Elevation contours adapted from *The Times Atlas of
the World,* seventh comprehensive edition (New York:
Times Books, 1985).

5   6   7   8   9   10   –   JR   –   96   95

Independent Picture Service

Coastal areas have been continuously thrashed by wave action, which has produced some interesting and unusual rock formations. This strange stone is located near a cluster of Indian caves.

Contents

Introduction **5**

1) The Land **8**
Topography. Climate. Flora and Fauna. Waterways. Natural Resources. Cities.

2) History and Government **17**
Discovery and Settlement. Foreign Attacks. The Nineteenth Century. U.S. Possession. Luis Muñoz Marín. Commonwealth Status. Government.

3) The People **33**
Population and Society. Health. Religion. Education. Recreation. Festivals. The Arts. Housing. Migrant Workers.

4) The Economy **48**
Industrial Development. Agriculture and Mining. Tourism and Regionalism.

Index **64**

ATLANTIC OCEAN

Aguadilla
Puntilla
Arecibo
Arecibo R.
Culebrinas R.
Añasco R.
Utuado
Mayagüez
Adjuntas
Lake Yauco
San Germán
Yauco R.
Ponce
Fort Allen
Guánica Bay

El Morro
SAN JUAN
Sabana
Seca
Communications Center
Hato Rey
Loiza
Aldea
Río
Piedras
Carolina
Bayamón
Guaynabo
Mameyes
Fajardo
Ceiba
Car. Nat. For.
Luquillo Div.
Fort Bundy
Roos
Roads Nava
Barranquitas
La Plata R.
Cayey
Humacao
Yabucoa
Salinas Army Training Center
Guayama
Chuco R.
Bayamón R.

CARIBBEAN SEA

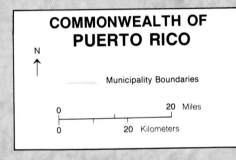

COMMONWEALTH OF PUERTO RICO

N ↑

Municipality Boundaries

0 — 20 Miles
0 — 20 Kilometers

Culebra Is.
Virgin Passage
Mona Passage
PUERTO RICO
Vieques Is.
Mona Is.

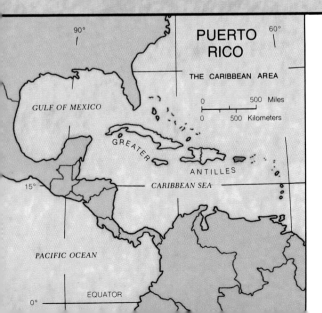

PUERTO RICO

90°   60°

THE CARIBBEAN AREA

0 — 500 Miles
0 — 500 Kilometers

GULF OF MEXICO

GREATER

ANTILLES

CARIBBEAN SEA

15°

PACIFIC OCEAN

EQUATOR

0°

METRIC CONVERSION CHART
To Find Approximate Equivalents

WHEN YOU KNOW:	MULTIPLY BY:	TO FIND:
AREA		
acres	0.41	hectares
square miles	2.59	square kilometers
CAPACITY		
gallons	3.79	liters
LENGTH		
feet	30.48	centimeters
yards	0.91	meters
miles	1.61	kilometers
MASS (weight)		
pounds	0.45	kilograms
tons	0.91	metric tons
VOLUME		
cubic yards	0.77	cubic meters
TEMPERATURE		
degrees Fahrenheit	0.56 (*after* subtracting 32)	degrees Celsius

In *The Hacienda of the Dawn,* Puerto Rican artist Francisco Oller y Cestero depicted the tall chimney stack of an abandoned sugar mill in about 1894. A few years later, the island would become a U.S. protectorate.

Introduction

Few topics spark a livelier debate among Puerto Ricans than the issue of the precise relationship between Puerto Rico and the United States of America, with whom the island is "freely associated."

To understand this discussion, it is necessary first to recall 450 years of Puerto Rican history. Under Spanish rule, Puerto Rico evolved into a colony devoted to sugarcane growing and cattle raising. Its prosperity, however, was interrupted by the frequent attacks of lawless pirates sailing the Caribbean who often pillaged the island and its inhabitants.

Spanish influence sank deep roots, and Puerto Ricans adopted many customs from their conquerors, but they also developed a dislike for Spanish colonial government. Spanish colonists abused the people of the island, exploiting their labor, reaping their harvests, and keeping the earnings for themselves.

Signs of change came only in the final years of Spanish rule. Liberals in Spain were persuaded to review Puerto Rico's case for greater local government, a case brought by the islanders to Spain. With Puerto Rico's willing assistance, Spain

5

fashioned a new charter for its colony that might in time have led to a form of Puerto Rican self-rule. But a powerful neighbor—the United States—became involved.

As a result of the Spanish-American War of 1898, Puerto Rico became a possession of the victorious United States. Puerto Ricans were confronted with learning another language and with adapting to a new culture. Most Puerto Ricans lacked the skills and education necessary to deal with these changes.

Although Puerto Ricans welcomed the benefits of U.S. rule, including improved health care and roads, they disliked that the island's resources continued to be exploited by those who governed it from far away.

In the mid-twentieth century, Puerto Ricans became increasingly uneasy about their disadvantages. Violence might have broken out had not Luis Muñoz Marín—Puerto Rican poet, writer, and diplomat—been on the scene. Muñoz Marín arranged to make Puerto Rico a commonwealth of the United States in 1952. The change of status from colony to commonwealth

Inadequate housing has long been a problem in Puerto Rico. Since achieving commonwealth status in 1952, the island has built many new dwellings—some of which reflect a Spanish influence in their architectural design.

Eight enthusiasts perform a native island dance during the Le Lo Lai Festival, which takes its name from a traditional refrain often heard in old Puerto Rican music.

meant that Puerto Ricans would have more control over their government and would maintain only loose political ties with the United States. The agreement satisfied an overwhelming majority of Puerto Rican citizens.

Puerto Rico has progressed under its own leaders since the 1950s. The commonwealth spends a large proportion of its budget on education, but many of its most promising graduates seek job opportunities on the mainland. To help offset the job shortage, the government has shifted the economy from farming to manufacturing. The transition has nearly eliminated major agricultural exports—mainly sugarcane, tobacco, and coffee. As Puerto Ricans adjust to the changes industrialization has brought to their traditional lifestyle, they also struggle with the question of commonwealth versus statehood.

An enhanced commonwealth, which the Popular Democratic party favors, gives the islanders greater self-government but without the burden of paying federal income taxes. Statehood supporters, championed by the New Progressive party, believe that the poorest Puerto Ricans would benefit by receiving their fair share of welfare payments and social services.

In November of 1993, Puerto Ricans voted on a referendum to retain their commonwealth status. Since statehood was defeated by such a narrow margin, many Puerto Ricans consider the debate still on. Puerto Rico's fate lies in the hands of its citizens as the island continues to grow and change.

A sixteenth-century seawall surrounds the grounds of the governor's residence, called La Fortaleza (the fortress). At this pier in centuries past, Spanish officials and high church dignitaries were welcomed ceremoniously to Puerto Rico.

Rolling hills and green shrubbery are typical features in the topography of the southwestern part of Puerto Rico.

1) The Land

From near Key West, Florida, almost to South America runs a rugged chain of submerged mountains whose highest peaks have pushed above the water to form an irregular chain of islands known as the West Indies. Within the West Indies group, the Greater Antilles comprises Cuba, Jamaica, Hispaniola (Haiti and the Dominican Republic), and Puerto Rico. Puerto Rico is the easternmost and the smallest of the Greater Antilles and lies 1,050 miles from the tip of Florida. North of the island is the Atlantic Ocean. To the south is the Caribbean Sea. The Virgin Passage separates Puerto Rico from the U.S. Virgin Islands to the east. The Mona Passage separates the western end of the island from the Dominican Republic.

Approximately 100 miles long and 35 miles wide, the island has an area of 3,515 square miles, which is smaller than the state of Connecticut. More than three million people live in this compact region, with an average of 1,083 inhabitants to each square mile—a population concentration greater than Britain's and 15 times that of the United States.

Three sizable islands—Mona, off the west end of the main island, and Culebra and Vieques, off the east end—are among a number of islands that dot Puerto Rico's coastal waters. Most of Vieques—once called Crab Island—has been owned by the U.S. Navy since the 1940s and is used for maneuvers with live ammunition. There is a strong movement in Puerto Rico to force the navy to give up control of the island.

Both the U.S. Navy and the U.S. Army have several installations on the main island. The navy's Sabana SECA Communications Center is on the coast west of San Juan, and its naval station at Roosevelt

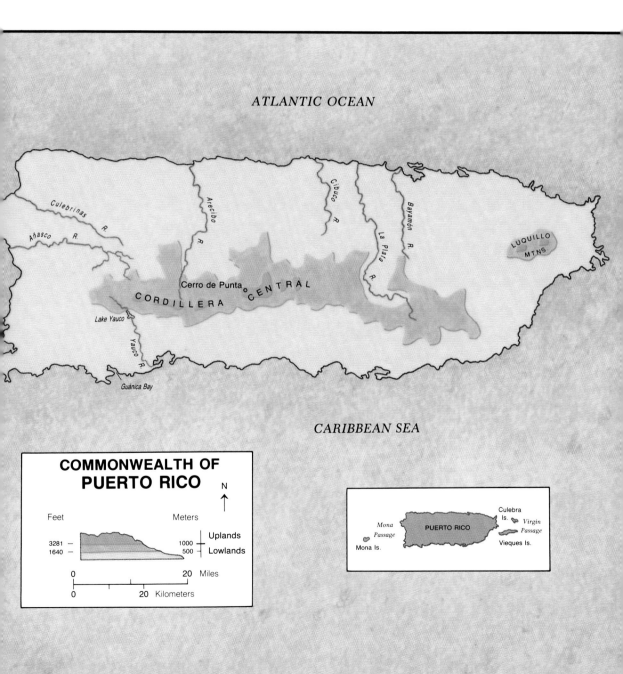

ATLANTIC OCEAN

Culebrinas R.

Añasco R.

Arecibo R.

Cibuco R.

La Plata R.

Bayamón R.

LUQUILLO MTNS

Cerro de Punta

CORDILLERA CENTRAL

Lake Yauco

Yauco R.

Guánica Bay

CARIBBEAN SEA

COMMONWEALTH OF PUERTO RICO

N

Feet | Meters

3281 — | 1000
1640 — | 500

Uplands
Lowlands

0   20   Miles

0   20   Kilometers

Mona Passage

Mona Is.

PUERTO RICO

Culebra Is.

Virgin Passage

Vieques Is.

An aerial view of the U.S. naval station at Roosevelt Roads in northeastern Puerto Rico shows its large airfield. The base also has extensive port facilities, since it juts out into Vieques Sound near the islands of Vieques and Culebra. The station is the most important U.S. base in the Caribbean and is home to the Atlantic Fleet Weapons Training Facility.

Roads, including Fort Bundy, is near Ceiba on the northeast coast. Fort Allen and the Salinas Training Area are U.S. Army sites in south central Puerto Rico.

Topography

The contours of the Puerto Rican landscape resemble a crumpled piece of stiff paper, with jagged peaks, steep valleys, and uneven plains. Two volcanic mountain chains ripple across the island. The larger chain is the Cordillera Central and forms a west-to-east backbone in the interior. A smaller chain, the Luquillo Mountains, occupies Puerto Rico's northeastern corner. The highest peak, Cerro de Punta, rises to a height of 4,389 feet, towering over the narrow, fertile valleys that interlace the mountains.

Encircling the island is an extensive coastal plain once used by early Spanish settlers for cattle grazing but now largely devoted to sugarcane plantations and cattle ranching. The southern portion of the coastal plain must be irrigated to raise crops, but elsewhere on the island thousands of small streams that crisscross the mountains provide a good water supply. The mountains, once covered by tropical rain-forests, today are mostly bare and rocky. This deforestation is the result of centuries of erosion and extensive logging operations that produced ceiba—or silk cotton, the official commonwealth tree—cedar, ebony, magnolia, laurel, mahogany, and West Indian sandalwood in great quantities. The government is now replanting forests on federally owned land, and officials encourage Puerto Ricans to do the same on privately owned land.

Climate

The temperature of Puerto Rico is remarkably stable throughout the year. Daytime averages range from about 75° F in the winter to 80° F in the summer. Although the days are generally quite warm, fresh breezes sweep down from the mountains to make the nights pleasantly cool.

Puerto Rico averages 65 inches of rain annually; no other part of the United States, except Hawaii, has more precipitation. Summer and autumn are rainy seasons, but most moisture comes in the form of light showers. It is a rare day when the sun does not shine at least part of the time.

Independent Picture Service

Many streets on the island are lined with tall, graceful palm trees, which are common throughout the tropics.

U.S. Navy Photograph, PHC Gotauco

Deforestation on a large scale reveals Puerto Rico's bumpy topography.

The island lies in the hurricane belt of the Caribbean. More than once, hurricanes have devastated the area. In 1979 Hurricane David struck Puerto Rico, the Dominican Republic, and the southeastern United States. In 1985, after three days of rains, about 150 Puerto Ricans were buried in a mud-and-rock slide at Mameyes. Hurricane Hugo struck eastern Puerto Rico in September 1989. Hugo's winds destroyed homes, buildings, and crops, causing $1.1 billion in damages. Because of the advance warnings available through meteorological equipment, precautions are now taken to keep damage and loss of life to a minimum.

Flora and Fauna

There are no poisonous or dangerous wild animals on the island. The reinita, the commonwealth bird, is a common migratory warbler with a gray head and yellow body that is found throughout the island. Mongooses were brought in to control the rat population on the sugarcane plantations, and native mammals and reptiles are represented by turtles, iguanas, and a few species of bats. The coquí—named for its loud, two-note nocturnal song (*ko-kee*)—is a small tree frog found almost nowhere

Birds of all kinds flock to the sanctuary of the Luquillo Division of the Caribbean National Forest where abundant greenery offers these animals a welcome perch.

Eleutherodactylus portoricensis is the scientific name of this tiny frog. Its name—literally free-fingered Puerto Rican one—tells us that its toes are not webbed together. On the island this shy amphibian is called a coquí and is usually found on moist foliage.

The flamboyant, also called the royal poinciana, is a fairly common tree in the tropics. Tens of thousands of its flowers burst into crimson, yellow, or orange-yellow blossoms at the same time, creating a lacy, parasol effect.

else in the world. The frog's powerful voice belies its size—one and a half inches—and it has a remarkable ability to cling upside down to tree leaves and moist foliage, as well as to change color from black to beige for protection from the sun.

The destruction of forested land—the natural habitat of the coquí—nearly wiped out some tropical species. The Puerto Rican parrot was nearing extinction when scientists stepped in to help increase its population by building artificial nests in protected areas to attract the parrots and incubating (artificially warming) parrot eggs. Protected areas and national parks also help to ensure that plants and wildlife are preserved.

Remains of the once-lush rain-forest can still be found at the Luquillo Division of the Caribbean National Forest (also called El Yunque) that also serves as a bird sanctuary. Located in the northeastern section of the island, El Yunque (the Anvil) receives 135 inches of annual rainfall and has roughly 240 tree species within its boundaries. Bamboo trees, leafy ferns, red-blossomed poincianas, orchids, coconut palms, and many flowering trees—such as hibiscus and African tulip—add vivid beauty to the island. Orange, mango, avocado, papaya, and other fruit trees can be found growing wild, and bananas, pineapples, grapefruit, guavas, and breadfruit are also cultivated in Puerto Rico. The lush valleys were once covered with sugarcane and tobacco, and the tillable slopes of the mountains are generally the site of coffee plantations.

Waterfalls are hidden throughout the Luquillo Division's protected rain-forest—also called El Yunque—which is located high in the mountains of northeastern Puerto Rico.

13

Guests at Camp Garcia, a naval base on Vieques Island where amphibious maneuvers are practiced, relax under a palm tree on the beach.

Along the coastal plains, white-sand beaches graced by backdrops of tropical greenery curve in and out along the sea's edge. They provide a scenic setting for sunbathing, diving, and swimming. The coastal waters abound with tuna, Spanish mackerel, lobster, mullet, barracuda, kingfish, and oysters.

Waterways

Puerto Rico has no rivers that are navigable by large vessels. The Arecibo River is the longest waterway. Smaller waterways such as the Yauco, Añasco, Bayamón, Cibuco, Culebrinas, and La Plata rivers are used for irrigation and as local sea-lanes. Lake Yauco—one of the island's land-bound bodies of water—has been dammed to provide Puerto Rican buildings with hydroelectricity.

Natural Resources

Spain's concerted exploitation of the gold deposits in Puerto Rico left the island depleted of this metal. There are, however, large deposits of copper in Adjuntas and Utuado, as well as lesser amounts of limestone, cobalt, chromium, nickel, and iron ore. Clay, peat, and glass sand (used in the island's bottle industry) are also found.

Cities

The cities in Puerto Rico present a picturesque and unusual contrast between old Spain and the modern world. Towering new buildings of steel-and-glass construction stand among the classical Spanish architecture. Wide, heavily traveled avenues intersect the many narrow, winding streets that meander through the older sections of Puerto Rico's cities.

SAN JUAN

San Juan, on the north coast, is the capital and the largest city (population 449,000). Originally, the Spanish made it a walled city, and much of it—called Old San Juan—can still be seen today. Old San Juan features narrow streets paved with the blue-gray blocks once used to stabilize Spanish ships. The Institute of Puerto Rican Culture has preserved many of San Juan's churches and mansions, including La Fortaleza, now the governor's palace, built between 1533 and 1540. It is the oldest government building in the United States. Juan Ponce de León, the first Spanish governor of the island, is buried in the sixteenth-century cathedral.

Independent Picture Service

Modern San Juan is a bustling metropolis with all of the amenities – fine restaurants, major hotels, and splendid beaches – that might be expected of a coastal capital city.

Courtesy of Puerto Rico Federal Affairs Administration

There is another side to San Juan, too. With the help of the Institute of Puerto Rican Culture, many of the capital's old colonial buildings have been carefully restored and preserved for future generations to enjoy.

Guarding the coastal approach to San Juan is El Castillo de San Felipe del Morro—commonly called El Morro—reputedly the strongest Spanish fortress in the New World. The fort was begun in 1539 and was continually refortified until the late eighteenth century. Its strategic position and forbidding construction successfully repelled English and Dutch attacks. A second fort, San Cristóbal, was built in the seventeenth and eighteenth centuries to defend the landward side of San Juan.

SECONDARY CITIES

Three inland cities—Bayamón (population 222,000), Guaynabo (93,000), and Carolina (178,000)—are within 10 miles of the capital. Their residents commute to one or another city to work or shop. Ponce (188,000) to the south, Arecibo (93,000) in the north, and Mayagüez (100,300) to the west are the other principal cities. After these municipalities, cities and towns decrease in size to countless tiny villages tucked around the mountains of the interior. Many of these small hamlets have less than 100 inhabitants.

Virtually every community in Puerto Rico can be reached by car on the network of modern highways that spreads across the island. More than 1.65 million vehicles are currently in use. There is no passenger railway system. Track is used only for freight. Many shipping lines make Puerto Rico a regular port of call, and 30 airlines maintain regular schedules between the United States and sprawling, modern San Juan International Airport or several smaller airports.

Independent Picture Service

Packed tightly together in Ponce—the southern coastal city that is third in size to San Juan—are the blazing white towers of Our Lady of Guadalupe Cathedral and the red-and-black *Parque de Bombas*. The latter building serves as both fire station and tourist information center.

These petroglyphs (carved line drawings on stone) are attributed to the pre-Columbian Taino Indians. The drawings were discovered at Utuado deep in the Puerto Rican interior.

Courtesy of Puerto Rico Federal Affairs Administration

2) History and Government

The early history of Puerto Rico is typical of the Caribbean region. The island was reached by Columbus, exploited by the Spanish, repeatedly attacked by the English and French, and used as a base by pirates and smugglers.

Discovery and Settlement

Called Boriquén (Land of the Valiant One) by its native Taino Indians, Puerto Rico (meaning "rich port" in Spanish) was ex-

plored by Columbus on his second voyage to the New World in 1493. He named the island San Juan Bautista (St. John the Baptist). Columbus sent cattle from the Spanish colony of Hispaniola (the present-day nations of Haiti and the Dominican Republic) to fatten them on the island's nutritious grasses. But the Spanish made no serious effort at colonization until 1508. In that year, Ferdinand II—king of Castile, Aragon (both part of modern Spain), and Sicily—sent Juan Ponce de León to

Only a few traces survive of the Indians who inhabited the island before its discovery by the Spanish. This ancient ceremonial ballpark was built at Utuado 700 years ago. The game played here, in which a bounced ball was kept in the air by hitting it with any part of the body except the hands, was observed by early Spanish settlers.

the island. A former foot soldier under Columbus, Ponce arrived with 50 armed men and an inhumane attitude toward the island's 30,000 Indians. He thirsted for gold and had grand ideas of adding another colony in the New World to the crown of Spain.

Initially, Ponce was successful. The Taino Indians—the Spanish called them Borinquéns—were part of the Arawak group. Although close cousins of the Caribs found throughout the Caribbean, the Taino lacked the Carib fierceness. The more peaceful group was subdued quickly and was put to work in the gold mines. By 1582 the Taino had been worked to exhaustion and soon disappeared altogether from the island's population.

The first Spanish settlement, Caparra, was founded inland from what is now the city of San Juan. In 1519, however, Caparra was relocated to the present and more-defensible site of San Juan and renamed La Ciudad de Puerto Rico. In about 1521—perhaps because of a cartographer's error—the city of Puerto Rico

Juan Ponce de León accompanied Christopher Columbus on his second voyage to the New World in 1493. Ponce claimed Puerto Rico for Spain and ruled it as its first governor from 1510 to 1512.

Stone steps lead up to the stately church of Porta Coeli (Gate of Heaven) in the main plaza of San Germán. Founded in 1511, this town is one of Puerto Rico's oldest settlements.

Built by Ponce's family in 1523, *Casa Blanca* (White House) was where the explorer's descendants lived for about 250 years. It later became the residence of the commander in chief of the military garrison on the island and is now a historical museum.

Puerto Rico's native population was cruelly enslaved by the Spanish conquistadors, who forced the Indians to dig for gold and to labor in the fields.

came to be called San Juan, and the island of San Juan came to be known as Puerto Rico. Except for a brief period from 1900 until 1932, when the island was mistakenly spelled "Porto Rico" by outsiders, its name has remained unchanged since the sixteenth century.

In the beginning, trade with Spain was brisk. Sugarcane was introduced from the Spanish colony of Santo Domingo (present-day Hispaniola) in 1515, and a few years later the first African slaves were brought to the island to do the work formerly handled by the Taino. With slavery the custom, agriculture flourished. Cotton, ginger, cacao, sugarcane, and indigo were cultivated and exported in small quantities. In the first years of Spanish settlement, a great deal of gold was mined.

Foreign Attacks

The success of the new colony, however, was to be short lived. The gold mines, which had seemed so promising, were soon

Britain's Sir John Hawkins died aboard his ship in the waters off the Puerto Rican coast while he and his kinsman, Sir Francis Drake, were attempting to take El Morro.

Famed throughout Europe for his daring raids on Spanish ports, Sir Francis Drake roamed the New World in search of ships to plunder and cities to take. The appearance of one of his ships, which flew the flag of Queen Elizabeth I, signaled danger to life and property.

The *Golden Hind* was Drake's most famous ship and was used for plundering as well as for exploring the New World. Formerly named the *Pelican,* the vessel was 75 feet long and had 18 guns.

depleted of their precious metal. Nevertheless, Puerto Rico seemed a rich prize to the European powers, who were fiercely competing to add overseas possessions to their empires. France, England, and the Netherlands tried to seize Puerto Rico from Spain. Until about 1580 the island was a target for French raiders. Striking mostly at unguarded settlements along the southern, western, and northern coasts, the buccaneers virtually stripped the island of its produce and cattle. These raids showed the Spanish the strategic importance of Puerto Rico, and this awareness led to its further fortification. For example, El Morro, which is still standing, is a massive Spanish fortress built to protect the port of San Juan.

The French attacks on Puerto Rico were followed by those of the English. In 1595 Sir Francis Drake and Sir John Hawkins, corsairs of Elizabeth I's court, launched a bloody but unsuccessful attack against El

Morro during which Hawkins died. Three years later, George de Clifford, the Earl of Cumberland, captured the fortress and held it for over six months. But in 1598 disease ravaged the attacking troops, which, combined with harassing counterattacks from the settlers, finally forced Clifford to withdraw.

Thirty years later, the Dutch tried to seize Puerto Rico. Bowdoin Hendrik landed with a large force in 1624 and laid siege to El Morro for several weeks before he and his fleet of ships from the Dutch West Indies Company were turned away.

Hendrik's attack was the last foreign invasion for over 100 years, but during the seventeenth and eighteenth centuries the settlers found themselves endangered from still another quarter—Spain itself. European powers prized their colonies as markets for goods produced in the mother country. Therefore, under Spanish rule, Puerto Rico was not allowed to trade with any other country except Spain, even though for years Spanish merchants had been bypassing the island to trade at other Caribbean ports.

French, Dutch, Danish, and British traders—barred from engaging in legal trade with the Puerto Ricans—turned to smuggling. They brought their goods into the agricultural settlements along the coasts that were safely distant from San Juan. Slaves, farm equipment, and cloth were

The Spanish conquerors of Puerto Rico began construction of El Morro in 1539; by the late eighteenth century the fortress had evolved into its present form. Built to guard San Juan from seaborne marauders, the fortress survived a short-lived occupation by the English in 1598 and a destructive fire set by the Dutch in 1624.

Cannons still stand at the ready through openings in the heavily fortified walls of El Morro.

Centuries of pounding surf and the corrosive effects of salty sea air have mottled the surface of El Morro's battlements. The British invasion in the late eighteenth century was one of the last attempts to take the fortress.

exchanged for Puerto Rican cattle, pigs, mules, ginger, tobacco, fruit, vegetables, and, after 1750, coffee. Although smuggling flourished and contributed to the island's agricultural growth, trade in San Juan slowed to the point of nonexistence.

The one profitable enterprise established in San Juan during the eighteenth century was piracy. Supported by Spain and acting under letters of marque (governmental permission to plunder the enemy), privateers from Puerto Rico began to raid the trade lanes of the Caribbean. For more than 50 years they operated with efficiency and a disregard for international law. Their activities stimulated the economy of San Juan during this period. As a result, privateers wielded a strong influence over the island and for many years played an active part in governing the colony.

In the late eighteenth century, Spain joined France in hostilities against Britain. Spanish and French privateers helped government troops repel a British force of 10,000 men who, under Sir Ralph Abercromby, laid siege to El Morro.

23

In this painting, Francisco Oller commemorated the inspiring work of Rafael Cordero, a modest tobacco worker of San Juan who provided free schooling to the children of slaves in the nineteenth century.

The Nineteenth Century

Abercromby's defeat was followed by nearly a century of relative peace and gradual improvement of social, economic, and political conditions. In 1808 Spain accorded Puerto Rico representation in the Spanish parliament. Alejandro Ramírez, a Spanish governor, took firm steps to abolish unauthorized trade in 1813, and Spain permitted Puerto Rico to conduct unrestricted trade with foreign ships in 1815.

This change meant that Puerto Rico was open to immigration and settlement, and thousands of settlers came to the island to develop the coffee, cotton, and cacao plantations. From a population of 155,000 inhabitants in 1800, Puerto Rico grew to 500,000 in 1850 and to 900,000 in 1898. Until 1873, when slavery was officially abolished, the newcomers imported black Africans to work the land.

In spite of Spain's gradual willingness to permit the Puerto Ricans to govern themselves, small rebellions occurred in 1835, 1838, 1867, and climaxed with El Grito de Lares (Cry of Lares) in 1868. To calm the situation, Spain accorded Puerto Rico the status of a province in 1869, and the islanders divided into two political groups. Those who were satisfied with Spanish rule joined the Conservatives. They opposed the Liberals, or Autonomists, whose goal was Puerto Rican self-rule under the protection of Spain.

Just as modern-day Puerto Rico is indebted to Governor Luis Muñoz Marín for its twentieth-century developments, nineteenth-century Puerto Rico was indebted to his father, Luis Muñoz Rivera—poet, newspaperman, statesman, and founder of the Autonomist party. Largely because of his negotiations with Spain's liberal prime minister, Práxedes Mateo Sagasta, Puerto Rico gained a substantial measure of independence during the latter part of the nineteenth century. Mateo Sagasta's Liberal Fusion party enacted the Autonomic Charter in 1897, which gave Puerto Rico virtual independence from Spain.

U.S. Possession

Whether Puerto Rico would have been unconditionally self-governing under the

Luis Muñoz Rivera worked tirelessly to improve relations between his fellow Puerto Ricans and their Spanish administrators. His efforts were nearly realized in the late nineteenth century, but they were interrupted by the Spanish-American War. Undeterred, he took up the cause again with the victor in the brief war—the United States—and managed to pressure Congress to extend the rights of his fellow islanders under the Jones Act of 1917.

Courtesy of Museum of Modern Art of Latin America

The Dominican Convent *(left)* and the church of San José *(right)* have undergone many changes since they were constructed in 1523 on land donated by the conquistador Juan Ponce de León. For more than a century, the convent was used as an arsenal. From 1898 to 1966, it was the headquarters of the U.S. Antilles Command, and today it is used by the Institute of Puerto Rican Culture as a museum.

charter was soon of little concern. On July 25, 1898, shortly after the outbreak of the Spanish-American War, U.S. troops under General Nelson A. Miles landed at Guánica Bay on the southern coast of Puerto Rico. The U.S. fleet under Admiral William T. Sampson bombed San Juan, and a few minor skirmishes occurred between the defending Spanish and the attacking U.S. troops. But the island fell with little resistance. In December of 1898, under the Treaty of Paris, Puerto Rico became part of the United States.

Two years of U.S. military rule in Puerto Rico followed the end of hostilities with Spain. In 1900 the U.S. Congress passed the Foraker Act, which set the pattern for the governance of the island as a U.S. colony.

The act allowed Puerto Ricans to elect only minor political figures. These included members of the lower house of the island's legislature and mayors and other city officials. The islanders also chose a resident commissioner, who could sit in the U.S. Congress in Washington, D.C., but who could not vote. The president of the United States appointed all other officials of Puerto Rico. Moreover, the U.S. Congress reserved for itself the right to annul acts approved by the Puerto Rican legislature.

The Foraker Act thus gave Puerto Rico much less freedom than did the Autonomic Charter of 1897 decreed by Spain. Furthermore, the islanders were not granted U.S. citizenship. Although the U.S. Congress considered it temporary, the act remained in effect for nearly two decades.

Reform was slow in coming. Islanders pressed for independence with the energetic support of Luis Muñoz Rivera. He had been

Among the island's achievements while it was a U.S. possession is its extensive road system, which ventures from coast to coast and throughout the interior.

Courtesy of Puerto Rico Federal Affairs Administration

Courtesy of Museum of Modern Art of Latin America

Puntilla (Little Point) near Arecibo was the last piece of soil occupied by Spanish troops in Puerto Rico after the Spanish-American War. Under the terms of surrender, the United States allowed the Spanish flag to fly at Puntilla until the last Spanish soldier embarked for his homeland.

resident commissioner in Washington, D.C., until his death in 1916. As a result of these efforts, Congress passed the Jones Act in 1917. This edict, which replaced the Foraker Act, granted U.S. citizenship to all Puerto Ricans and set up a two-house legislative assembly, the upper house of which was to be elected by the islanders. Yet the governor, key members of the cabinet, and all supreme court justices were still appointed by the U.S. president.

During the next 20 years, the U.S. government proved generous in providing funds to build dams, hospitals, roads, and schools. But U.S. business firms increasingly tightened their grip on the colony's economy. They bought the large plantations previously owned by the Spanish, and they operated the island's highly profitable sugar mills. Despite a provision restricting any corporation from holding more than 500

Joseph Foraker, U.S. senator from Ohio from 1897 to 1909, supported the policies of President William McKinley and introduced the first Organic Act to Congress in January 1900. Also called the Foraker Act, the initiative provided guidelines for civil government in Puerto Rico.

A large sugar refinery in Central Machete, near Guayama, is surrounded by acres and acres of tall, ripe sugarcane.

acres of land, four conglomerates managed to control more than 176,000 acres. Land reform was to become a major political issue on the island and was to shape much of its present form of government.

Luis Muñoz Marín

Puerto Ricans needed a dynamic, dedicated leader. They found one in Luis Muñoz Marín, whose father Muñoz Rivera, had led the island toward political freedom in the late nineteenth and early twentieth centuries. Following his father's death in 1916, Muñoz Marín remained on the U.S. mainland, making a name for himself as a poet and writer of political commentary for influential U.S. periodicals. By the time he returned permanently to Puerto Rico and joined the newly founded Liberal party, Muñoz Marín could count on the support of

highly placed officials in the new administration of President Franklin D. Roosevelt.

The Liberal party proved to be divided, and its members often worked at cross purposes. In 1938, therefore, Muñoz Marín organized the Popular Democratic party (*Populares*) with a platform—embodied in the slogan "Bread, Land, Liberty"—that emphasized economic reconstruction and land reform. Muñoz Marín encouraged his fellow Puerto Ricans to join him in dealing with the island's immediate social and economic problems and to postpone the issue of status under U.S. colonial rule. In 1940, on the eve of World War II, Muñoz Marín and his party won a victory by a slim margin, gaining control of the island's senate and achieving equality with an opposition party in the lower chamber.

Once in office, the Populares set up an industrial planning board, a transportation

Raised in New York City and Washington, D.C., Luis Muñoz Marín shared his father's literary and journalistic talents, as well as his active interest in Puerto Rician politics. Before entering the governor's mansion, Muñoz Marín edited *La Democracia,* a liberal newspaper founded by his father. After four terms as governor, he became an elected member of the Puerto Rican Senate.

29

Pan, Tierra, Libertad, or "Bread, Land, Liberty," was the motto on the political posters of the newly formed *Populares,* whose party platform—largely developed by Luis Muñoz Marín—called for extensive agrarian (land) reform.

department, and a housing authority. The civil service was strengthened, and the Water Resources Authority was reorganized. For the first time, the United States enforced the section of the Jones Act limiting corporations and partnerships to owning no more than 500 acres of Puerto Rican land. Under "Operation Bootstrap," as the Populares dubbed their economic reorganization plan, the island gradually began to struggle successfully against the oppressive weight of poverty.

Commonwealth Status

Impressed by Puerto Rico's progress, the U.S. Congress passed a bill—conceived by Muñoz Marín and his friends within the mainland Democratic party—to create the Commonwealth of Puerto Rico (*Estado Libre Asociado* in Spanish). The bill was signed by President Harry S. Truman on August 5, 1947. With this special status, Puerto Rico could elect its own governor and—as an underdeveloped part of the United States—could enjoy special economic advantages.

Muñoz Marín was elected Puerto Rico's first governor in 1948 and was reelected in 1952, 1956, and 1960. His first task as governor was to convince other Puerto Ricans that their territory should become a commonwealth of the United States. He succeeded, by a margin of nearly five to one, in 1952. Acceptance of commonwealth status was not accomplished without disagreements. Disgruntled Puerto Ricans who favored independence attempted to assassinate President Truman, killing a White House policeman in the process.

Since 1960 power in Puerto Rico has shifted between two major parties. The Populares want Puerto Rico to remain a commonwealth, while the New Progressive party advocates statehood for Puerto Rico.

A third party, the Puerto Rican Independence party, favors complete self-rule for the island. Some supporters of independence have sought to achieve their goals through violence. The Fuerzas Armadas de Liberación Nacional (Armed Forces of National Liberation) exploded several bombs in U.S. cities in the 1970s and 1980s. Another Puerto Rican terrorist group, the Macheteros, also backs independence. They have directed their violence primarily against U.S. military personnel stationed on the island.

In the early 1990s, the U.S. Congress reviewed several bills to change Puerto Rico's status. The two main political parties

Courtesy of Meredith Pillon/Puerto Rico Tourism Company

At El Morro, the flags of the United States (left), **Puerto Rico** (center), **and San Juan** (right) **fly together.**

Courtesy of Puerto Rican Tourist Company

La Fortaleza, the governor's mansion, was begun in 1533 as a fortress. It soon became evident that the site was not in a good defensive position, so the stronghold was developed into a lavish residence, which was greatly expanded in the nineteenth century. It is the oldest governmental house in continuous use in the Western Hemisphere.

each lobbied for their point of view, causing the bill to languish. In late 1991, the islanders defeated a measure that supported commonwealth over statehood. In November 1993, however, the referendum to remain a commonwealth won by a slim margin of 48 percent to 46 percent. Another 6 percent of the voters supported complete independence, indicating that the issue of Puerto Rico's status remains unresolved.

Government

The Commonwealth of Puerto Rico is governed by its own constitution and by the Federal Relations Statute. The statute consists of parts of the Jones Act of 1917 that remained in force after the creation of the commonwealth.

The island's legislative assembly is made up of a senate and a house of representatives, whose members are elected by direct vote every four years. Eight senatorial districts elect 2 senators each, and 40 representative districts choose 1 representative each. Whenever one political party controls more than two-thirds of the seats of either house, the minority party receives extra at-large seats—up to 11 additional seats in each house. Puerto Rico has a resident commissioner in the U.S. Congress who gives advice but who can vote only in committee. The islanders hold U.S. citizenship but cannot vote in national elections unless they move to the mainland.

Executive power is vested in a governor elected by direct vote to a four-year term. There are 15 executive departments, each headed by a secretary who is appointed by the governor. The 15 secretaries form the governor's cabinet.

The judiciary system consists of a supreme court comprised of a chief and associate justices, who serve until they reach 70 years of age and who are appointed by the governor. The district court judges are appointed to eight-year terms.

Courtesy of Puerto Rico Federal Affairs Administration

The bicameral (two-house) Puerto Rican Legislative Assembly meets under the dome of the capitol, surrounded by the blue waters of San Juan Bay. Construction of the building began in 1925 under Puerto Rican architect Rafael Carmoega. The offices of senators and representatives flank either side of the dome.

Puerto Rican families tend to be large in number, and a strong emphasis is placed on education from an early age.

3) The People

Puerto Rico's ethnic makeup is diverse. Few people with Indian ancestry remain, and intermarriage between whites and blacks has been common since the Europeans imported the first slaves in the early sixteenth century. As the centuries passed, other groups were added to the tiny island's heritage.

The upper class is predominantly of Spanish ancestry. Most Puerto Ricans, however, are a mixture of European, Indian, and African backgrounds. Indo-European populations generally live in the mountains, while Afro-European groups tend to be found on the coasts.

Population and Society

In the mid-1990s, 3.7 million people lived in Puerto Rico. Seventy-three percent resided in urban areas—a reversal of a trend that had lasted for over 400 years. Population density is much higher in Puerto Rico than it is in the United States.

Nearly one-third of the islanders are younger than the age of 15, compared to one-fifth on the mainland. The island also has a higher rate of population growth than does the United States. This means that more Puerto Ricans are being added to the island's educational and health systems. In addition, as more young

33

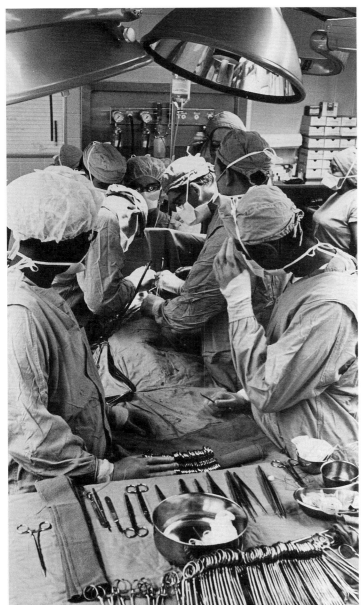

A surgical team is in the midst of an operation at the 3,400-bed Puerto Rico Medical Center in Río Piedras, near San Juan. The longevity of Puerto Rican residents has risen dramatically in the past few decades as commonwealth standards of living, nutrition, and medical facilities have improved.

Courtesy of Commonwealth of Puerto Rico

people seek jobs, the pressure to create employment increases.

In economic terms, Puerto Rico has two distinct groupings of citizens. The gap is wide between the small number of San Juan aristocrats, who speak both English and Spanish, and the Spanish-speaking majority. The island's wealthy people are well educated and highly placed through-

out the government. They have little difficulty switching from the Hispanic culture of Puerto Rico to the English-speaking culture of the mainland United States.

Most Puerto Ricans speak only Spanish with ease. Rural workers, called *jibaros* on the island, are usually the least educated and struggle to make ends meet. The poorest citizens of the island live in slums that surround the largest cities. From this low-income majority come most of the emigrants to the mainland.

Puerto Rican leaders hope that greater industrialization will answer emigration, employment, and poverty problems. Since the 1960s, many jibaros have become factory laborers, a change that requires a cultural as well as an economic transition.

Health

Among the benefits that Puerto Ricans have enjoyed as part of the United States is an improvement in the health-care system. Until the twentieth century, health facilities were inadequate or nonexistent. In addition, a poorly balanced diet left most people undernourished.

With commonwealth status, these aspects of life on the island have changed. Modern medicines have nearly eliminated malaria, once one of Puerto Rico's most serious diseases, and have sharply reduced cases of tuberculosis. In 1940 the average Puerto Rican could expect to live to the age of 46. In the mid-1990s, that figure was 74. Infant mortality—the number of newborns who die within the first year of life—has also dropped to 13 deaths in every 1,000 live births.

Courtesy of Economic Development Administration of the Commonwealth of Puerto Rico

These bilingual professionals are members of Puerto Rico's modern financial sector.

Courtesy of Commonwealth of Puerto Rico

For the low-income jibaro, government-sponsored, housing—such as this project at Río Piedras—has relieved some of the problems caused by poor sanitation and by the high incidence of preventable disease.

Independent Picture Service

Jibaros have historically been employed as agricultural manual laborers – in the delicate job of picking the ripest coffee beans, for example.

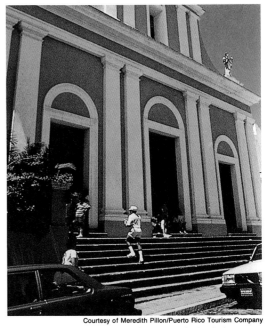

Courtesy of Meredith Pillon/Puerto Rico Tourism Company

Believers attend services in San Juan Cathedral.

Religion

Eighty percent of Puerto Ricans consider themselves Catholic. For the jíbaro, however, spiritualism holds a strong place in island beliefs, and the ancestral religions of the Indians and the Africans are still powerful. Most low-income Puerto Ricans have been baptized formally in the Catholic Church.

Protestantism, unknown on the island prior to its occupation by North Americans, is fairly well represented. In order to prevent overlapping of effort, Protestant missionaries divided the island into zones, which still separate the different Protestant branches. The Baptists occupy a broad diagonal strip that runs across the island from Ponce to San Juan. The Methodists are located in the north near Arecibo. The western end of the island is heavily Presbyterian, and the eastern end is Congregationalist. The United Brethren are located on the south coast, and the Episcopalians are mainly in the large cities and suburbs.

Independent Picture Service

Other people from this same low-income group – such as this textile worker at Olympic Mills – have made the adjustment to the industrial labor force.

36

Dressed in neat, trim uniforms, two children head for classes at their neighborhood elementary school down one of Puerto Rico's many narrow, cobbled streets.

The cathedral at Humacao, a city of 20,000 inhabitants in the eastern part of the island, serves those of the Roman Catholic faith. Although about four-fifths of all Puerto Ricans are formally considered Catholics, a smaller number actually practice the religion.

Islanders have strong family ties and traditionally come from large families. In many of the smaller villages, almost all of the inhabitants are related.

Education

All Puerto Ricans speak Spanish, and many of them are also fluent in English. Spanish is the language of instruction in the schools, but English is taught and emphasized at all levels. Until 1948 English was the official language of instruction and was regarded as a symbol of colonialism. In 1948, however, the United States relinquished control of Puerto Rico's educational system and permitted the governor to appoint a commissioner of education. The commissioner was directly responsible to the governor and to the citizens of the island. Thereafter, education improved rapidly.

School enrollment increased by more than 40 percent between 1960 and 1983. In the mid-1990s, 95 percent of school-aged children attended classes. The literacy rate improved from 69 percent in 1940 to 90 percent in the mid-1990s.

Puerto Rico is also proud of its three large universities. Catholic University is located in Ponce and has 15,000 students. The University of Puerto Rico (53,000 students), founded in 1903, has most of its colleges at Río Piedras but also has campuses in Mayagüez, San Juan, Ponce, Arecibo, Cayey, and Humacao. The Inter-American University has several campuses located in Barranquitas, Fajardo, Hato Rey, and and Ponce and has a total enrollment of 46,700 students.

Universities commonly hold a full schedule of evening classes for the convenience of those who must work during the day. Recent years have witnessed an increase

In the school playground at recess, exuberant boys manifest Puerto Rico's new optimism. By the early 1990s, public schools of the commonwealth boasted an annual elementary-level enrollment of 432,000 pupils and a secondary enrollment of 483,000 students.

Students who arrive at the Río Piedras campus of the University of Puerto Rico walk along a palm-tree-lined road, which leads to the imposing Roosevelt Belltower of the central administration building.

A young Puerto Rican girl gracefully performs the *bomba,* a traditional African dance.

of smaller colleges on the island, many of them specializing in business, electronics, and technology for student bodies ranging in enrollment from about 500 to 3,000 pupils.

La Gaceta de Puerto Rico, the island's first newspaper, began publishing in 1807. Presently, there are three main Spanish-language dailies: *El Nuevo Día, El Reportero,* and *El Vocero.* The English-language newspaper is the *San Juan Star.*

Recreation

Puerto Ricans love sports, particularly baseball, horse racing, basketball, and cockfighting. Gambling is popular too—the national lottery is a considerable source of income for the island. Anywhere, anytime, a cockfight is bound to draw an excited crowd, and good fighting birds are only slightly less well known than outstanding baseball players. Among the more famous Puerto Rican athletes is Roberto Clemente. An outfielder with the Pittsburgh Pirates, Clemente died in a 1972 airplane disaster just after takeoff from San Juan International Airport.

Making handicrafts is another popular pastime. Many Puerto Ricans are skilled artisans and fashion beautiful objects from native woods, seeds, clays, and fibers. Puerto Rican homes are decorated with handmade pottery, straw rugs, and baskets.

Born in Carolina, Puerto Rico, in 1934, Roberto Clemente had an impressive .414 batting average in the 1971 World Series. Named most valuable player for the series, he died one year later in a tragic plane crash.

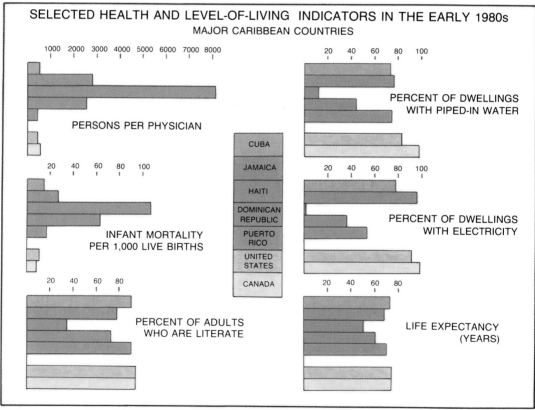

Artwork by Carol F. Barrett

This graph shows how greatly each of six factors, which are suggestive of the quality of life, varies among the five major Caribbean countries. The United States and Canada are included for comparison. (Data from *UN Statistical Yearbook 1982, 1984 UN Demographic Yearbook, 1986 Britannica Book of the Year,* and "1986 World Population Data Sheet.")

Festivals

The heritage of old Spain is felt not only in the language and architecture of Puerto Rico but also in the island's strongly rooted culture. Spanish influence is everywhere—in music, art, drama, and literature. From the Spanish, too, come the many fiestas that are such an integral and joyful part of Puerto Rican life. The feast days of the Catholic Church are widely observed and, more often than not, are the occasion for citywide or villagewide celebrations, pageants, and parades.

The Feast of St. John the Baptist, for whom the island was originally named by Columbus, is one of the most enthusiastically celebrated festivals of the year. For several days before and after the actual feast day (June 24), there are parties, carnivals, dances, and music in the colorfully decorated plazas. On the night of June 23, thousands of families keep all-night vigils before open bonfires on the beaches. At dawn, they wade into the water in a symbolic reenactment of the baptism of Jesus. This act of piety, according to Puerto Rican tradition, assures the islanders of good health for the coming year.

Each town has its own patron saint, and each saint's day is another occasion for a long, loud, and happy festival. Churches hold special services on a saint's day, and often a procession of worshipers will wind through the streets carrying candles, holy relics, and statues.

At Christmas, Puerto Ricans combine Spanish, North American, and local customs. As a result, the Christmas season starts in early December and continues through January 8.

Puerto Rican music and dancing reflect the influences of a long Spanish history, with flamenco-style moves and traditional costumes.

Masked revelers parade through the streets during festival time in Loíza Aldea, a seacoast village east of San Juan.

Bright lights strung from pillar to post bedeck the main plaza of Arecibo, northern Puerto Rico, during the pre-Lenten Carnival celebrations.

At Loíza Aldea, a craftsperson prepares the festive masks that will be worn throughout the local Festival of St. James on July 25.

Children receive gifts on both *Noche-buena* (Christmas Eve) and on Three Kings' Day (Epiphany), which is celebrated on January 6. Santa Claus takes care of the gift giving on Nochebuena. On Three Kings' Day children put boxes of fresh grass under their beds for the camels of the wise men. By the next morning, according to tradition, the camels have eaten the grass, and toys and candy have been left in its place.

Throughout Christmastime, groups of singers and musicians wander from house to house singing villancicos, or Christmas carols. Traditional Christmas dishes include *arroz con dulce,* a sweet rice pudding; different kinds of sausages; and *pasteles,* a banana paste mixed with chopped meat and wrapped in plantain leaves. Perhaps the favorite Christmas treat is *lechón asado,* lean pig roasted whole over a bed of glowing charcoal.

Other local dishes are *asopao* (mixed stew) and *yuquiyú* (rice, sausage, pineapple, and peppers cooked in a pineapple husk). Yuquiyú is named after the ancient Indian god who reigned over the rainforest and protected the island and its people.

Pablo Casals – Spanish cellist, composer, conductor, and pianist – received his first musical instruction from his father and made his performance debut in Paris in 1898. After leaving his homeland in 1939 following the Spanish civil war, Casals resided in France. He moved to San Juan in 1956 and died at Río Piedras in 1973, at the age of 96.

The Arts

Music flourishes in Puerto Rico. The works of Puerto Rican composers range from the nineteenth-century folk dances of Juan Morell Campos to the modern pieces of Rafael Hernández, which are known throughout Latin America.

The great cellist Pablo Casals, a Spaniard, came in 1956 to make his home in Puerto Rico, the island of his mother's birth. It was the 84-year-old Casals who established the Puerto Rico Symphony Orchestra and Commonwealth Conservatory in 1960 for Puerto Ricans who wished to study music. The Casals Festival, held each spring, is one of the best known musical events in the world. It has featured musicians such as Isaac Stern, Jan Peerce, Alexander Schneider, and Eugene Istomin.

As in Spain, the most popular form of literary expression in Puerto Rico is poetry. The island has many poets, several of whom are famous in the Spanish-speaking world. Eugenio María de Hostos, one of Latin America's greatest thinkers, was born near Mayagüez in 1839. A philosopher and judge, he wrote on such subjects as history, sociology, logic, and political economy. He also authored children's books.

Among Puerto Rico's most famous poets is José Gautier Benítez, whose poetry often deals with the beauty of the Puerto Rican landscape. The poet died at the early age of 29, but his artistic colleague Francisco Oller preserved his memory in this nineteenth-century portrait.

Courtesy of Museum of Modern Art of Latin America

Since the nineteenth century, Puerto Rican literature has followed social and political themes. Manuel Pacheco Alonso preserved the speech and customs of the jíbaro, and Alejandro Tapia y Rivera wrote works like *The Quadroon Women,* which deals with racial prejudice. Puerto Rico's social problems and fiery politics became motifs in the romantic poetry of José Gautier Benítez, José de Diego, and Manuel Zeno Gandia. A political protest magazine, *La Revista de las Antillas,* appeared in 1913 and gave voice to much of

Puerto Rico's frustration and desire for change. Throughout the 1930s, books such as Antonio Pedreira's *Insularism* and Tomás Blanco's *Historical Summary of Puerto Rico* attempted to define the island's identity. The post–World-War-II writers Enrique Laguerre, José Luis Gonzáles, and Pedro Juan Soto choose themes for their fiction that deal with the Puerto Rican experience in New York City.

Among Puerto Rican painters, the nineteenth-century works of José Campeche and Francisco Oller y Cestero are well known. As an ardent abolitionist, Oller produced vibrant works that mirrored his antislave sentiments and depicted the natural wonders of the native land he loved.

Puerto Rico has also produced fine actors, including José Ferrer and Juano Hernández. Opera stars of stature have included Graciela Rivera and Justino Diaz.

The Puerto Rican government, which has worked diligently to improve the economic and political status of the island, has also taken organized steps to raise the cultural standards of its citizens. Under a project called *Operación Serenidad* (Operation Serenity), a traveling library and a mobile museum go from town to town on the island, and a theater on wheels brings drama to the out-of-the-way villages.

The Ponce Museum of Art was founded in the southern coastal city by former governor Luis A. Ferré. The museum was designed by Edward Durell Stone—architect of New York City's Museum of Modern Art—and exhibits U.S. and European art from the past five centuries.

A still life by Francisco Oller depicts Puerto Rico's tasty dwarf bananas alongside cashew nuts, which grow in bean-shaped shells on tropical evergreen trees.

A crowd gathers to watch a live performance by Theater on Wheels, a traveling troupe that brings dramatic works to less-frequented areas of the island.

Courtesy of Commonwealth of Puerto Rico

One of the most effective agencies of Operación Serenidad is the Institute of Puerto Rican Culture. Established in 1955 to study, promote, and preserve the island's traditional culture, the institute has offices throughout the island. The institute sponsors concerts, lectures, ballets, art exhibits, plays, and films.

Housing

In any small country in which overpopulation and mass poverty go hand in hand, housing is a serious problem. Puerto Rico is no exception. Today, however, *bohíos*—palm-thatched cabins built on stilts—and the zinc-and-wood homes of the urban poor are being replaced with modern housing at minimal cost. The government supplies materials and technical aid to families grouped into home-building cooperatives. The cooperative members do the actual construction themselves. Of the 60,000 houses built between 1950 and 1960, about 10,000 were put up this way.

The self-made house is built of reinforced concrete or concrete blocks and consists of a living room, two bedrooms, and a kitchen. The cost is extremely low and is paid in small monthly installments over periods of up to 10 years. In government-encouraged housing, rents are determined by family size and income. An apartment for a family with seven children may be had at a low rental rate. Puerto Rican housing planners are confident that eventually most of the slum areas will be replaced by attractive, low-cost housing.

In recent years, crime and drug trade have invaded government-subsidized housing communities. The Puerto Rican Public Housing Authority (PRPHA) has had to spend funds intended for the repair of decaying public housing on building fences and guardhouses and on training public housing police. As a result, the PRPHA has set up a long-term plan to renovate public housing over the next six to seven years to improve living conditions.

Migrant Workers

Thousands of Puerto Rican migrant workers go to the United States annually to work on farms in the east and midwest during the harvest season. They later return to the island to help handle the Puerto Rican harvest.

The island government neither encourages nor discourages its citizens from going to the United States. Once the islanders have migrated, they find that the commonwealth has established agencies in New York and other cities to help them get settled as quickly as possible.

Puerto Ricans who move to the U.S. mainland have to face many of the same social barriers that confront newcomers from other countries. Cultural differences and language problems present serious difficulties, and black Puerto Ricans have to surmount the additional obstacle of racial discrimination. Prejudice based on skin color is a new situation for the Puerto Rican. On the island, whites and blacks have lived together in relative peace for four centuries. Despite their difficulties as newcomers, Puerto Ricans contribute a great deal to the mainland's economy.

In recent years, Puerto Ricans who have remained on the mainland have become a voice for change on the island. Second-generation Puerto Ricans have consistently represented New York City in the U.S. Congress. Many mainland Puerto Ricans maintain close ties with the island and want to be able to vote on issues that directly affect Puerto Rico's commonwealth status.

Independent Picture Service

Public housing of all sorts—government sponsored, low cost, and large scale—has appeared in many of the island's urban centers.

Cruise ships touring the Caribbean regularly stop at San Juan.

4) The Economy

Because of Puerto Rico's unique status as a commonwealth, Puerto Rico's economy has features shared by no other territory under the U.S. flag. The government of the island is much more involved in economic decision making than are the governments of the 50 states. This practice results from the island's need to modernize and to enhance economic and educational opportunities.

Commonwealth status has given Puerto Rico several advantages that were designed to speed up the island's economic development. For example, Puerto Rican citizens pay no federal taxes. And to encourage mainland industries to locate branches on the island, the Industrial Incentives Act (1947) gave a 10-year tax exemption to new companies willing to invest in Puerto Rico.

While the Industrial Incentives Act has been amended over time, it has continued to stimulate development on the island. Threatened by U.S. cuts in government spending, such favorable tax breaks are likely to be reduced or eliminated. However, Puerto Rico has many assets such as a solid infrastructure, a well-trained work force (especially in high-tech industries), and a fast-growing tourist industry. Foreign and U.S. industries will likely continue to invest in Puerto Rico.

Puerto Rico's economy thus exhibits two sides in its operation. On the one hand,

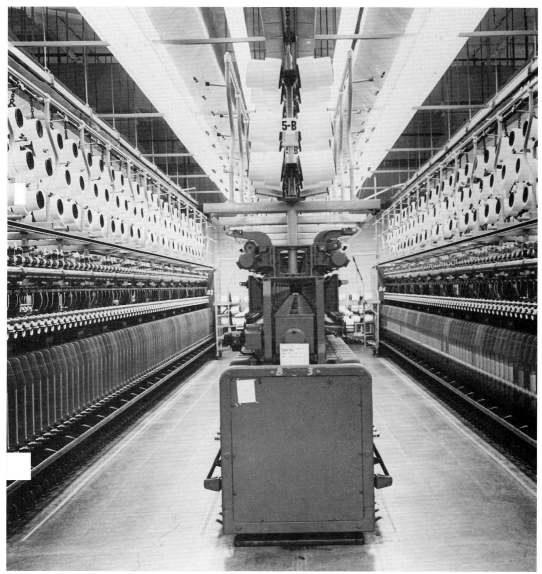

Phillips Petroleum, a mainland U.S. corporation, has located a subsidiary, Fibers International, at Guayama on Puerto Rico's southern coast. Manufacturing is now the primary contributor to the island's GDP and provides 168,000 jobs. The main products—pharmaceuticals, electrical and electronic equipment, petrochemicals, processed food products, textiles, clothing, and Puerto Rican rum—contribute more than $13 billion to the island's economy.

49

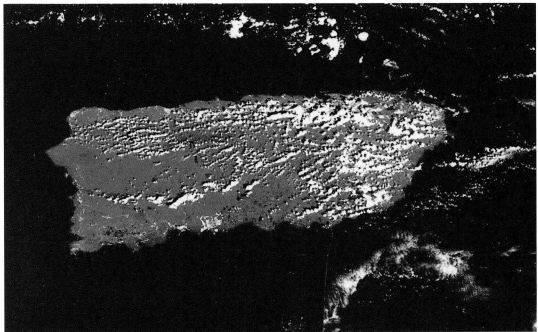

Courtesy of National Aeronautics and Space Administration

A passing U.S. satellite composed a computerized image of Puerto Rico and its resources. The red coloring indicates forests or green cover, the gray tufts represent clouds, and the black clusters mark cities and towns.

like any state, Puerto Rico uses the U.S. dollar as currency, trades its goods within all areas of the United States without restriction, and is subject to fluctuations in the overall U.S. economy.

On the other hand, unlike individual states, Puerto Rico can participate in legislation favorable to the interests and welfare of its citizens by lobbying in Washington, D.C. Similarly, Puerto Rico must try to prevent the passage of laws that might damage its economy. The main lobbyist is the island's resident commissioner, who works to gain the general support of members of Congress. As a rule, the commissioner seeks to ensure that Puerto Rico is included as a recipient of federal programs that benefit low-income people—such as food stamps. At the same time, the commissioner also seeks to avoid the impact of measures that might work hardships on Puerto Ricans—such as paying taxes for improvements that would benefit the mainland, but not Puerto Rico.

Independent Picture Service

The Water Resources Authority uses helicopters to erect transmission poles. In 15 days 119 poles were put up using this method—a job that would have taken ground crews five months to complete.

Industrial Development

Industrial development in Puerto Rico began with Operation Bootstrap, an outgrowth of Governor Luis Muñoz Marín's scheme drawn up in the 1940s. It was designed by Puerto Ricans for Puerto Rico and set the pattern for the island's economic and social reconstruction.

The first step was the creation of a Planning Board in 1942 to serve as a clearinghouse and an organizing agency for the entire self-help project. The Planning Board decided on priorities, set specific goals, and generally administered one of the most successful economic reorganizations in history. The actual details of the scheme were handled by three other boards, the Water Resources Authority, the Government Development Bank, and the Economic Development Administration.

The Arecibo Observatory, where scientists study such astronomical phenomena as pulsars and gas clouds, is the largest radio telescope in the world. Its reflector is a 20-acre curved bowl installed in a deep, natural sinkhole. New York State's Cornell University operates the telescope for the National Science Foundation.

Lacking its own petroleum resources and without a sufficient number of damable rivers, Puerto Rico operates many thermal plants *(above and below)* **that consume imported fuel to produce roughly 98 percent of the island's electricity. The remaining percentage is produced by a few hydroelectric installations. More than 13 billion kilowatt hours of electricity are produced annually.**

The Government Development Bank has encouraged the construction of large-scale housing projects – such as the three developments seen in this aerial view of a region just outside of San Juan.

The Water Resources Authority (now called the Puerto Rico Electric Power Authority) developed a power system that enabled the island to industrialize. In 1940 electrical output was only 130 million kilowatt hours; in 1964 more than 3 billion kilowatt hours of electrical energy were produced. During the last three decades, this figure has risen to more than 13 billion kilowatt hours.

The Government Development Bank is concerned primarily with the government's monetary arrangements. It supervises loans from the government to private industry by acting as a negotiating agent for private investors. It has been effective particularly in spurring private builders to produce large-scale housing projects for low- and middle-income families.

The Institute of Puerto Rican Culture has had a hand in preserving, restoring, and reusing run-down colonial-era buildings in old San Juan. El Convento is now a hotel but – as its name implies – was once a Roman Catholic convent. Currently the renovated chapel is used as the dining room.

53

Perhaps the most important government agency, however, is the Economic Development Administration, known to Puerto Ricans as *Fomento* (meaning promotion, encouragement, or aid). Fomento encourages foreign companies to invest in Puerto Rico and is responsible for the flow of private capital into the island.

Fomento began by building and operating factories until they were well established, then selling them to private investors. It obtained tax exemptions for industry and promoted the island to outside manufacturers as a good site for factories. To bring in the industry it wants, Fomento makes economic studies, locates plant sites, arranges for construction of buildings, and provides engineering and marketing advice. In some cases, it will even train personnel.

Fomento's success has been remarkable. In Puerto Rico, branches of U.S. corporations manufacture clothing and textiles, such as lingerie, hosiery, gloves, and shoes. Other industries produce pharmaceuticals, chemicals, copper wire, fasteners, and light meters. Precision bearings, transistors, cameras, television sets, and optical lenses are also manufactured.

Fomento is credited with establishing more than 2,000 factories on the island. They employ about 150,000 people—18 percent of the total Puerto Rican labor force. This industrial thrust has caused a fundamental change in Puerto Rico's economy, which agriculture once dominated. By the mid-1990s, farming represented only about 1.4 percent of Puerto Rico's money-earning sectors, while manufacturing accounted for about 40 percent of the island's economic activity.

Courtesy of Puerto Rico Federal Affairs Administration

Recent years have seen a revival of Puerto Rico's reputation for producing high-quality rum, which is made from the juice or syrup of sugarcane at a bottling plant operated by the Bacardi Company.

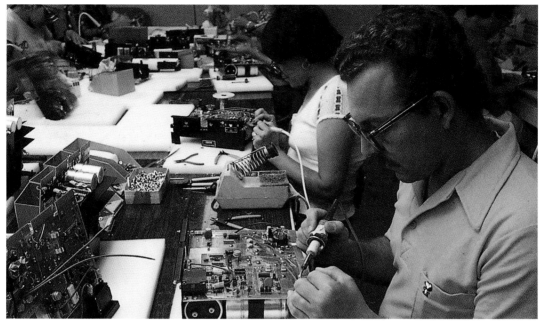

Puerto Rico's electronics industry may help to stem the flow of commonwealth citizens to the mainland in search of jobs.

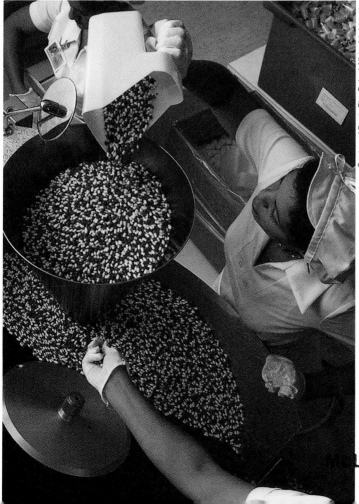

Pharmaceuticals are among the products manufactured by U.S. corporations that have plants in Puerto Rico. The corporations seek to capitalize on special tax incentives as well as on the island's plentiful supply of labor.

55

McLean County Unit #5
105 - Carlock

The backbreaking work of sugarcane harvesting is evident as laborers cut the cane by hand. Sometimes this task is accomplished by machines.

Once the cane stalks have been cut, they are gathered together for transport—in this case via secondary railway track—to a sugar mill for processing.

56

Agriculture and Mining

Because only one-third of Puerto Rico is farmable, agricultural land has been jealously guarded. Many farms operate on a small scale and feed only those who work on them. Currently, the average size of a farm is 34 acres, while only 6.2 percent of the holdings are of 100 or more acres.

Despite the need to create jobs in areas other than agriculture, which cannot provide enough employment, critics of Operation Bootstrap believe that the program de-emphasized farming too quickly. Sugarcane produers, for example, eventually were struggling to survive.

In the 1960s, the Puerto Rican government bought almost all of the sugar mills and most of the crop land from their owners. But there are currently only two refineries in use, and the production of sugarcane, once the island's largest export, has fallen fairly steadily to a record low. In a peak season during the early 1950s, Puerto Rico produced nearly 1.4 million tons of raw sugar. By the 1990s, the harvest was less than 74,000 tons.

Puerto Rico once exported tobacco and coffee on a large scale. These crops are now

Independent Picture Service

Despite complaints that Operation Bootstrap quickly took Puerto Rico out of the agricultural mainstream and into industrialization, some technological advancement on the farming front has been accomplished. Here, tomatoes are grown employing a hydroponic system, which uses nutrient-rich, chemically treated water – instead of soil – as the cultivation medium.

grown mostly for local consumption. An average of 14,000 tons of coffee and 200 tons of tobacco are produced each year.

Independent Picture Service

Like sugarcane cutting, pineapple harvesting is a slow, laborious process. Each fruit must be cut from the plant by hand. Workers then take the pineapples from the fields in baskets carried on their heads.

Agricultural activity in Puerto Rico centers on the dairy, livestock, and poultry businesses. These contribute 1.4 percent to the commonwealth's gross domestic product (GDP), the value of all goods and services produced in a country within a year. Recently, the island has increased its harvest of avocados, coconuts, pineapples, oranges, and plantains (greenish, starchy bananas) that are grown for the local market.

Because sugarcane cultivation is no longer very profitable, experimental farms have turned to raising corn, soybeans, and other grains. Using new technologies in drip irrigation, Puerto Rican farmers are growing melons, tomatoes, squash, pumpkins, peppers, eggplant and other fruits and vegetables. Cocoa has been successfully introduced in a few regions, and some low-lying sugar-growing areas have been replanted with rice.

Mining has a small place within the Puerto Rican economy. Roughly 10,000 workers are employed in producing stone, sand and gravel, and lime. More than 1.4 million tons of cement were made annually in the mid-1990s. Most of this output came from factories in San Juan and Ponce.

Courtesy of Minneapolis Public Library and Information Center

Sparsely branched papaya trees thrive in Puerto Rico's tropical climate and are exploited as much for their milky latex (used in meat tenderizers) as for their juicy fruit. Individual papayas can weigh as much as 20 pounds.

Tourism and Regionalism

Of continuing importance to Puerto Rico is its rapidly rising tourist trade. The year-round sunshine, extensive white-sand beaches, and the tropical lushness of most of the island attract about 3.9 million visitors a year. More than half are from the mainland United States. Tourists bring in more than $1.6 billion annually, contributing 69 percent to the island's GDP.

The Caribe Hilton, one of the first major tourist hotels on the island, was built by the government at a cost of more than $7 million and then leased to the Hilton International Corporation to manage. Opened in 1949, the hotel, through its tourist earnings, paid back the government's entire investment by 1957. Hotels and resort facilities are now numerous along the beaches and in the mountains.

The growth of manufacturing and tourism in Puerto Rico has turned the

Independent Picture Service

Choice tobacco is hand picked on hillside farms for curing under natural conditions in sheds. The bulk of the crop is harvested from December through March each year.

Courtesy of Puerto Rico Federal Affairs Administration

Most of San Juan's large hotels are located in clusters in the Condado or Isla Verde sections of the city. A carefully drawn government plan created an attractive – but concentrated – area for tourism.

Courtesy of Puerto Rico Federal Affairs Administration

Some of the best scuba diving in the Caribbean can be done in the clear, deep waters surrounding Puerto Rico, where a rich and varied sea life thrives.

59

This tricot mill in Arecibo manufactures women's hoisery. The plant employs more than 500 workers.

Sun Oil is a $125 million complex in Yabucoa, southeastern Puerto Rico. The plant processes crude oil into naphtha (used in solvents), jet fuel, and kerosene.

A further part of Puerto Rico's expanding industrial base is its production of aluminum materials.

continental United States and its island commonwealth into mutually beneficial customers. On a per capita basis, Puerto Rico buys more from the United States than does Canada or several substantially larger Latin American nations. In turn, Puerto Rico benefits too, for the mainland United States is the island's best client.

Puerto Rico has made several attempts—with only limited success—to promote increased trade and economic ties with its neighbors in the Caribbean. The commonwealth has participated in several now-defunct Caribbean organizations aimed at creating regionally integrated economies. Despite these failures, some Puerto Ricans believe that the island will make substantial progess only if it develops into the industrial center of the Caribbean.

Part of the attraction of a Caribbean market connection is that Puerto Rico, with its untaxed trade with the U.S. mainland, could link other Caribbean islands to U.S. markets. In this role as a middle agent, Puerto Rico could benefit its Caribbean neighbors and at the same time strengthen its own economy by widening its markets.

Money sent back to Puerto Rico by mainland immigrants provides the island economy with needed capital. These revenues were welcome during the recession

Part of Puerto Rico's close relationship with the United States is seen in the large number of navy and army installations located throughout the island. Here, Canadian vessels, which will participate in a joint exercise called Operation Safe Pass, wait at a naval station near San Juan.

Taking a shopping cue from the mainland United States, Puerto Rico built the **Plaza Las Americas** in San Juan as a multistoried mall, where long rows of shops attract both browsers and buyers.

that affected the U.S. economy in the 1980s and early 1990s. Unemployment on the island currently is 16.7 percent of the labor force. Approximately 60 percent of the population, however, lives below the poverty level.

Despite setbacks, Puerto Ricans remain confident about the future. Puerto Rico's transition from agriculture to manufacturing has provided more and better jobs for the island's work force. Although fewer crops are exported, the local market for goods has grown, as Puerto Ricans have more money to spend in their own communities.

Many islanders look forward to the day when they will no longer have to depend on federally funded programs to enable their economy to compete with those of other parts of the United States. Until then, Puerto Rican leaders—whether for the commonwealth or for statehood—seek to maintain the island's cultural identity while forging ahead with economic plans.

In a colonial-era home in Old San Juan, residents use ropes to bring food and other goods to the upper floors. The Puerto Rican government has made progress in saving old, crumbling buildings from destruction. Instead, the structures are restored for use as homes, restaurants, and museums.

Mainlanders from the United States pause to watch a fisherman repair his nets.

A cruise ship docked in San Juan harbor underscores Puerto Rico's interest in developing tourism and is in view of the Legislative Assembly building *(in the background).*

Index

African influence, 33, 36, 39
African slaves, 20, 22, 24, 33
Agriculture, 7, 10, 13, 20, 23, 36, 47, 54, 56–58, 62. *See also* Coffee; Sugarcane; Tobacco
Airports, 10, 16, 40
Architecture, 6–7, 14–16, 32, 41, 45, 53, 62
Arecibo, 16, 36, 38, 42, 51, 60
Arts and handicrafts, 5, 17, 24, 40–42, 43–46
Atlantic Ocean, 8
Autonomic Charter, 25–26
Beaches, 14–15, 41, 58–59
Caribbean National Forest, Luquillo Division, 12–13
Caribbean Sea, 5, 8, 12, 17, 22–23, 48, 59, 61
Casals, Pablo, 43
Castillo de San Felipe del Morro, El. *See* El Morro
Cathedrals and churches, 14, 16, 19, 26, 36–37
Cities, 14–16, 28, 36–38, 42–43, 49, 60. *See also* Arecibo; Ponce; San Juan
Climate, 11–12, 58
Coffee, 7, 13, 23–24, 36, 58
Columbus, Christopher, 17–18, 41
Communications, 29, 39, 44
Constitution, 32
Corporations, U.S. (in Puerto Rico), 28–30, 49, 55
Cuba, 8
Culebra Island, 9–10
Dance, 6, 39, 41
Deforestation, 10–11, 13
Dominican Republic, 8, 12, 17
Drake, Sir Francis, 20–21
Drama, 44–46
Economic Development Administration, 51, 54
Economy, 7, 22–24, 29–30, 34, 47–63
Education, 6–7, 24, 33, 37–39, 48
Electricity, 14, 50, 52–53
Electric Power Authority. *See* Water Resources Authority
El Morro, 16, 20–23, 31
England. *See* Great Britain
Erosion, 3, 10
Exports, 7, 20, 57–58, 62
Ferré, Luis A., 45
Festivals, 6, 41–43
Fish and sea life, 2, 14, 59, 63
Flora and fauna, 8, 10–14, 45
Fomento. *See* Economic Development Administration
Food, 43
Foraker, Joseph, 28
Foraker Act, 26, 28
Forestry, 10–11, 50
Fortresses, 7, 14, 16, 20–24, 31
France, 17, 21–23
Fruit, 13, 23, 57–58

Gold, 14, 18, 20–21
Government, 5, 7, 22–23, 29–30, 32, 35, 45–47
Government Development Bank, 51, 53
Governors, 18, 25, 28–32, 38, 45
Great Britain, 16–17, 21–23
Greater Antilles, 8
Guánica Bay, 26
Haiti, 8, 17
Hawkins, Sir John, 20–22
Health, 6, 33–35, 41
Hispaniola, 8, 17, 20
History, 17–32
  colonization, 5–7, 17–24
  commonwealth, 6–7, 30–32, 34–35, 38, 48, 61–62
  discovery and conquest of, 17–18, 20
  independence movement, 30–32
  nineteenth century, 5–6, 24–25
  U.S. possession, 25–32
Holidays, 43
Holland. *See* Netherlands
Housing, 6, 30, 35, 46–47, 53, 62
Hurricanes, 12
Imports, 61
Indians, 3, 17–18, 20, 33, 43. *See also* Taino
Industry, 7, 30, 35–36, 48–49, 51–55, 57–58, 60–61, 62–63
Infant mortality rate, 35
Institute of Puerto Rican Culture, 14–15, 26, 46, 53
Jíbaro, 34–36
Jones Act, 25, 28, 30–31, 32
Languages, 6, 34–35, 38–39, 41, 47
Legislative assembly, 28, 31–32, 63
Literacy, 38
Literature, 41, 43–44
Livestock, 5, 10, 17, 21, 23, 58
Maps and charts, 4, 9, 40
Mayagüez, 16, 38, 43
Military installations, U.S., 9–10, 14, 26, 61
Mining, 14, 58
Mona Island, 8
Mona Passage, 8
Mountains, 8, 10, 13, 16, 33, 58
Muñoz Marín, Luis, 6, 25, 29–30, 51
Muñoz Rivera, Luis, 25–26, 29–30
Museums, 19, 26, 45
Music, 6, 43, 45–46
Natural resources, 6, 14, 50, 52
Netherlands, 21
Operación Serenidad, 45–46
Operation Bootstrap, 30, 51, 57
Organic Acts. *See* Foraker Act; Jones Act
Painters, 5, 24, 44–45

People, 33–47
  characteristics of, 5–7, 33, 36, 38, 40–41, 47, 62
  as immigrants to U.S. mainland, 7, 34–36, 47, 55, 61–62
  standard of living, 6, 15, 30, 34–36, 46–47, 50, 62
  as U.S. citizens, 26, 28, 32, 62
Pirates and smugglers, 5, 17, 22–23
Political parties, 7, 24–25, 29–32
Ponce de León, Juan, 14, 17–19, 26
Pónce, 16, 36, 38, 45, 58
Population, 8–9, 14, 24, 33–35, 46, 61
Ports, 10, 15–16, 61
Protestantism, 36
Puerto Rico
  as commonwealth, 6–7, 30–32, 34–35, 38, 48, 61–62
  constitution of, 32
  economic advancement of, 7, 30, 48, 50–51, 53–54, 58, 62
  government of, 5, 7, 31–32
Rainfall, 11, 13
Rain-forests, 10, 13, 43
Ramírez, Alejandro, 24
Rebellions, 24
Religion, 36–38, 41. *See also* Protestantism; Roman Catholicism
Resident commissioner, 26, 28, 32, 50
Río Piedras, 34–35, 38–39, 43
Rivers and streams, 10, 14, 52
Roads, 6, 11, 14, 16, 27
Roman Catholicism, 36–37, 41, 53
San Juan, 2, 9, 14–16, 18, 20–24, 26, 31–32, 34, 36, 38, 42, 48, 53, 58–59, 61–63
Santo Domingo, 20
Spain, 5, 10, 14, 16–18, 20–27, 43
  as colonial power, 5, 14, 20, 22–24
  influence of, 5–7, 14, 20, 22, 33, 38, 41, 43
Spanish-American War, 6, 25–27
Sports and recreation, 2, 14, 18, 39–41, 59
Sugarcane, 5, 7, 10, 12–13, 20, 28, 47, 54, 56–58
Taino, 17–18, 20
Tax exemptions, 48, 50, 54–55
Textiles, 36, 49, 60
Tobacco, 7, 13, 23, 58
Topography, 3, 8, 10–11, 14
Tourism, 14, 16, 49, 58–59, 63
Trade, 22–24, 61
Transportation, 16, 56
Truman Harry S., 30–31
United States, 5–8, 11–12, 14, 16, 25–36, 38, 47–51, 58, 61–62
Universities, 38–39
Urbanization, 34–35

Vieques Island, 9–10, 14
Virgin Islands, U.S., 8
Virgin Passage, 8
Volcanoes, 10
Water Resources Authority, 30, 50–51, 53
West Indies, 8
Writers and poets, 7, 25, 29, 43–44
Yauco, Lake, 14